THE NEGATIVE USE OF THE WORD "BLACK" AND THE
PSYCHOLOGICAL AND RACIAL IMPLICATIONS IT
CONNOTATES

THE NEGATIVE USE OF THE WORD "BLACK" AND THE PSYCHOLOGICAL AND RACIAL IMPLICATIONS IT CONNOTATES

by

Lillian Victoria Knowles

Foreword by
Nova M. Edwards

Published by
Nova M. Edwards
lvknowlesbook@yahoo.com

ISBN-13: 978-0-9913892-0-9
ISBN-10: 0-9913892-0-4

TABLE OF CONTENTS

FOREWORD

When I was a child, it seemed like my mother Lillian, the author of this book, was always busy writing papers for school. As a requirement to obtain her Master of Arts in Social Science from California State University, Sacramento, my mother finished her last "paper" with her thesis *The Negative Use of the Word "Black" and the Psychological and Racial Implications It Connotates* in the summer of 1977. She explained to me how the word black has been used mostly in a negative way, and she wanted to explore the reasons and open the discussion to try to change that perception. She artfully presented her findings and arguments by using literary and historical examples in her thesis. Her thesis also addresses the psychological effects of the negative association of blackness and, conversely, the positive image of being black, such as during the Black Renaissance.

It was always her desire to expand and publish her thesis as a book. However, as most of us experience, time passes too quickly. Unfortunately, she was not able to publish her thesis before she died in December 1996. Therefore, this posthumous publication of Lillian Knowles's thesis is a fulfillment of her wish.

As this book was written in the 1970s, many of the publications used in the author's research precede that time. Therefore, there are racial terms and stereotypes in this book that today we would deem unacceptable and perhaps offensive. However, those terms were considered acceptable when the thesis was written and the author meant no harm when using them.

Also, this book is largely the same as the thesis with the exception of some minor edits, the removal of recommendations (as instructed by the author's hand-written notes), and the addition of an index.

Nova M. Edwards

Chapter One

INTRODUCTION

The intentions for investigating this problem is to bring awareness the way the word "black" is almost always used in a negative way. Interest and familiarity on this topic has led to a desire to explore the origin and reasons behind this type of negative thinking primarily in the West.

The approach used for this study was documentation. A sample of 75 books, magazines, periodicals and journals published in America were analyzed, reviewed and criticized to see how the word "black" is used in a derogatory way. Most of the material chosen for this study were of a scientific nature. Certain criteria were established for judging the books.

The examination of this topic has revealed some similarities among the culture of the West pertaining to the treatment of the negative image of black and the positive image of white. Relying solely on the books chosen for this study, it has been shown that this subject has evolved with new views and emphasis upon blackness starting from the mid-sixties.

It is the purpose of this study to put into perspective the negative aspect of the word "black." Since the negative use of the word "black" is so intertwined with that of various phases of black life throughout the entire history of the country, the vastness of the literature makes possible only a limited discussion of how black is used in certain texts.

The representative books on which the study is based were all written here in America. Included are texts written for general audience, secondary schools, and colleges. The majority of the books chosen appear to have been popular in their time and they include some books written by southerners as well as those of northerners. The selection of the books is arbitrary, but some care was taken to make it representative.

After examining the books, certain criteria were used to judge their range of relevant material. Abstracts were made of any points connected with the derogatoriness of black in American life. These, were arranged by topics and authors in order to study the material to the best advantage.

The purpose of this was to determine how black has been represented in these books. The study is an analysis of the traditional and changing treatments of black and the relationship it bears to blacks here in America.

The findings are organized into four chapters and two major time periods, pre-slavery and post slavery up to the 1960s. Each chapter is preceded by a brief summary, which sets the stage for the topics under discussion.

The analysis for the most recent period is especially numerous since accounts in books now in use formed the main basis for recommendations.

In view of the changes on the part of black Americans and the positive way that they now view black, attention has been given to some of the recent literature written by blacks and their perspectives on the problem are represented.

Although the primary interest centers on the nature of the reference to black as a negative term, other factors were also taken into consideration. The negative portrayal of Africa and Africans is discussed to show how black came to be a permanent negative adjective.

In the extent of treatment of topics, it should be kept in mind that the aim of this study is to present an unbiased view of the portrayal of black and blacks here in America and the way that blacks have chosen to deal with the problem. The ideal being striven for is a balanced presentation which will portray, as far as possible, the truth, with no idea of undue emphasis in order to counter-balance past neglect or distortion. The concentration upon so-called scientific books in no way denies the importance of the material in other books for the clarification of the subject.

The survey of recent writings on the negative usage of black is intended to serve two purposes. First, it should provide a background against which the accounts in school textbooks, scientific books and journals, and novels can be projected. Second, it forms part of the base on which later studies can be directed to eradicate this type of negative thinking.

For the purpose of this study, the following contentions are made:

1. Historically the term "Negro" was accepted by blacks because of the way Africa was portrayed and also because of the way that black was used.

2. The commonly held view that blacks hated themselves is false.

3. The current "black is beautiful" theme is not new. It had its roots in the early days succeeding slavery.

4. The symbolic reference to black and white is almost universal in the West.

5. The negative use of black can be found in most Western literature, including the Bible and the writings of William Shakespeare.

6. The primary origin of the modern color theme was first injected into our society by the earlier imperial powers.

The negative use of the word "black" probably had its origins in England. Chapter Two will discuss the effects the earlier imperial powers had upon this phenomenon as it is known today.

Chapter Two

HISTORICAL PERSEPCTIVE

In England the word "black" was used to connote unpleasant concepts. Blackness came to be associated with death, impurity, fear, uncleanliness, and evil, just as whiteness was associated with purity, victory, daylight, beauty, and virginity. Shakespeare, among others, glorified whiteness in Twelfth Night (1, 5, 210-222) and a Midsummer Night's Dream (II, I, 95 and III, 2, 141-144), and the dichotomy became embedded in the very fabric of the English language. As the British became involved with Africans, the nuances of their language contributed to the view that the black man was somehow a perversion of the positive images connoted by whiteness (Cortada, 1974, p 98).

The most arresting characteristic of the newly discovered African was his color. Travelers rarely failed to comment upon it; indeed when describing Africans they frequently began with complexion and then moved on to dress and manners. At Cape Verde, "These people are all blacks, and are called Negroes, without any apparell, saving before their privities." Robert Baker's narrative poem recounting his two voyages to the West African coast in 1562 and 1563 first introduced the Africans with these lines:

> And entering in (a river), we see
>   a number of blacke soules,
> Whose likelinesse seem'd men to be,
>   but all as blacke as coles.
> Their Captaine comes to me
>   as naked as my naile,
> Not having witte or honestie
>   to cover once his taile
>   (Hakluyt, 1958, "cited by" Jordan, 1968, p 132).

Even more sympathetic observers seemed to find blackness a most salient quality in Africans: "although the people were blacke and naked, yet they were civill" (Wren, 1566, "cited by" Jordan, 1968, p 270).

Englishmen actually described Africans as black which seemed to suggest that the African's complexion had a powerful impact upon their perceptions. Even the peoples of northern Africa seemed so dark that Englishmen tended to call them "black." Blackness became so generally associated with Africa that every African seemed a black man. In Shakespeare's day, the Moors, including Othello, were commonly portrayed as pitchy black and the terms Moor and Negro were used interchangeably (Cawley, 1938, p 31).

There was an inconsistency, however. Englishmen recognized that Africans south of the Sahara were not at all the same people as the much more familiar Moors. Sometimes they referred to these Africans as "black Moors" to distinguish them from the peoples of North Africa. During the seventeenth century the distinction became more firmly established and writers came to stress the difference in color, partly because Africans in West Africa were being taken as slaves and Moors were not. In the more detailed and accurate reports about West Africa of the seventeenth century, Africans in different regions were described as varying considerably in complexion. In England, the initial impression of Africans was not appreciably modified: the firmest fact about the African was that he was "black" (Jordan, 1968, p 6).

The powerful impact which the African's color made upon Englishmen must have been partly due to the suddenness of contact. Though the Bible as well as the arts and literature of antiquity and the Middle Ages offered some slight introduction to the "Ethiope," England's immediate acquaintance with black-skinned peoples came with relative rapidity. While the virtual monopoly held by Venetian ships in England's foreign trade prior to the sixteenth century meant that people much darker than Englishmen were not entirely unfamiliar, black men were virtually unknown except as vaguely referred to in the hazy literature about the sub-Sahara which had filtered down from antiquity. Native West Africans probably first appeared in London in 1554; in that year five Africans were taken to England, and according to the trader William Towrson, "kept till they could speake the language," and then brought back again "to be a helpe to Englishmen" who were engaged in trade with Africans on the coast. Hakluyt's later discussion of these Africans, who he said "could well agree with our meates and drinkes" though "the colde and moist aire doth somewhat offend them," suggests that these "blacke Moores" were a novelty to Englishmen (Hakluyt, 1589, "cited by" Jordan, 1968 p 176). In this respect, the English experience was markedly different from that of the Spanish and Portuguese who for centuries had been in close contact with North Africa and had actually been invaded and subjected by people both darker and more highly civilized than themselves. The impact of the African's color was the more powerful upon Englishmen because England's principal contact with Africans came in West Africa and the Congo where men were black; one of the fairest-skinned nations suddenly came face to face with one of the darkest peoples on earth (Jordan, 1968, p 7).

Viewed from one standpoint, Englishmen were participating in Europe's discovery that the men who were revealed by European expansion overseas came in a variety of colors. A Spanish chronicle translated into English in 1555 was filled with wonder at this diversity:

> "One of the marveylous thynges that God useth in the
> composition of man, is coloure: whiche doublesse can

> not bee consydered withowte great admiration on beholding one to be white and an other blacke, beinge coloures utterlye contrary. Sum lykewyse to be yelowe whiche is betwene blacke and white: and other of other colours as it were of dyvers liveres" (Arber, 1885, "cited by" Jordan, 1968, p 10).

As this passage suggests, the juxtaposition of black and white was the most striking marvel of all. And for Englishmen this juxtaposition was more than a curiosity.

In England perhaps more than in southern Europe, the concept of blackness was loaded with intense meaning. Long before they found that some men were black, Englishmen found in the idea of blackness a way of expressing some of their most ingrained values. No other color except white conveyed so much emotional impact. As described by the <u>Oxford English Dictionary</u>, the meaning of black before the sixteenth century included, "Deeply stained with dirt; soiled, dirty, foul . . . Having dark or deadly purposes, malignant; pertaining to or involving death, deadly; baneful, disastrous, sinister . . . Iniquitous, atrocious, horrible, wicked . . . Indicating disgrace, censure, liability to punishment, etc." Black was an emotionally partisan color, the handmaid and symbol of baseness and evil, a sign of danger and repulsion (Jordan 1 1968, p 120).

Embedded in the concept of blackness was its direct opposite-whiteness. No other colors so clearly implied opposition, "beinge coloures utterlye contrary": no others were so frequently used to denote polarization:

> Every white will have its blacke,
> And everye sweete its sowre (Willmott,
> 1857, p 27, "cited by" Jordan 1968).

White and black connoted purity and filthiness, virginity and sin, virtue and baseness, beauty and ugliness, beneficence and evil, God and the devil (Heather, 1948, p 59, "cited by" Jordan, 1968).

Whiteness carried a special significance for Elizabethan Englishmen particularly when complemented by red, the color of perfect human beauty, especially female beauty. This ideal was already centuries old in Elizabeth's time, (Curry, 1916, P 3, "cited by" Jordan, 1968) and their fair queen was its very embodiment: her cheeks were "roses in a bed of lillies." (Elizabeth was naturally pale but like many ladies then and since she freshened her "lillies" at the cosmetic table) (Wilson, 1939, p 337, "cited by" Jordan 1968). An adoring nation knew precisely what a beautiful queen looked like.

> Her cheeks, her chinne, her neck, her nose,
> This was a lillye, that was a rose;
> Her hands so white as whale's bone.
> Her finger tipt with Cassidone;
> Her bosome, sleeke as Paris plaster,
> Held upp twoo bowles of Alabaster.

Shakespeare himself found the lily and rose a compelling natural coalition.

> "Tis beauty truly blent, whose red and white
> Nature's own sweet and cunning hand laid on.
> (Shakespeare's Twelfth Night, The Complete
> Works of Shakespeare, 1954).

By contrast, the African was ugly, by reason of his color and also his "horrid Cules" and "disfigured" lips and nose. As Shakespeare wrote apologetically of his black mistress:

> My mistress' eyes are nothing like the sun;
> Coral is far more red than her lips' red;
> If snow be white, why then her breasts are dun;
>
> If hairs be wires, black wires grow on her head.
> I have seen roses damask'd, red and white,
> But no such roses see I in her cheeks
> (Harrison, 1933, p 64, "cited by" Jordan, 1968).

Some Elizabethans found blackness an ugly mask, superficial but always demanding attention.

> Is Byrrha browne? Who doth the question aske?
> Her face is pure as Ebonie jeat blacke,
> It's hard to know her face from her faire maske,
> Beautie in her seemes beautie still to lacke.
> Nay, she's snow-white, but for that russet skin,
> Which like a vaile doth keep her whiteness in
> (Harrison, pp 310~11, "cited by" Jordan, 1968).

A century later, blackness still required apology and mitigation; one of the earliest attempts to delineate the West African as a heroic character, Aphra Behn's popular story Oroonoko (1688) presented blacks as capable of blushing and turning pale (Behn, 1915, p 145, "cited by" Jordan, 1968). It was important that English discovery of black Africans came at a time when the accepted standard of ideal beauty was a fair complexion of rose and white. Blacks not only failed to fit this ideal but seemed the very picture of perverse negation (Thorndike, 1958, p 398, "cited by" Jordan, 1968).

From the first, many English observers displayed a certain sophistication about the African's color. Despite an ethnocentric tendency to find blackness repulsive, many writers were aware that blacks themselves might have different tastes. As early as 1621, one writer told of the "Jetty coloured" Africans, "Who in their native beauty most delight, and in contempt doe paint the devill white," this assertion became almost a commonplace and even turned up a hundred and fifty years later in Newport, Rhode Island (Heylyn, 1621, p 379, "cited by" Jordan, 1968). Many accounts of Africa reported explicitly that the African's preference in colors was inverse to the European's (Martyr, 1912, p 39, "cited by" Jordan, 1968). Even the African's features were conceded to be appealing to Africans. By the late seventeenth century, in a changing social atmosphere, some observers decided that the African's blackness was more handsome than the lighter tawny hues; this budding appreciativeness was usually coupled with expressions of distaste for "large breasts, thick lips, and broad nostrils," which many Africans "recokon'd the beauties of the country" (Moore, 1738, "cited by" Jordan, 1968, p 131). As one traveler admiringly described an African queen, "She was indifferently tall and well shap'd, of a perfect black, had not big lips nor was she flat nos'd as most of the natives are, but well featur'd and very comely" (Uring 1726, "cited by" Jordan, 1968, p 40).

By this time, the development of the slave trade to America was beginning to transform the African's color from a marvel into an issue. In what was a remarkable complaint for the master of a slaving vessel, Captain Thomas Phillips wrote in 1694 that he could not:

> imagine why they should be despis'd for their colour, being what they cannot help, and the effect of the climate it has pleas'd God to appoint them. I can't think there is any intrinsick value in one colour more than another, nor that white is better than black, only we think it so because we are so, and are prone to judge favourably in our own case, as well as the blacks, who in odium of the colour, say, the devil is white, and so paint him.

During the eighteenth century, the African's color was to come into service as an argument for "diversitarian" theories of beauty. Europe's discovery of "blacks" and "tawnies" overseas helped nurture a novel relativism. More important so far as the African was concerned, his color was to remain for centuries what it had been from the first, a standing problem for natural philosophers (Jordan, 1968, p 11).

Considered in a broader cultural context, it was the Africans' blackness which proved his most important characteristic. When he was not called a "Negroe" he was called by the indigenous term, a "black." Although the evidence from language and ideals of beauty in Elizabethan England suggests that the English response to blackness may not have been entirely a matter of associating a physical characteristic with social inferiority, the fact was that from the beginning white Englishmen met black Africans on a footing of inequality. Although Robert Pyle in 1698 suggests that repulsion for blackness may in some individuals have derived from deep levels in the personality which were associated with or perhaps even dependent upon purely physiological processes, the fact remains that Pyle perceived blackness in a specific and derogatory social context. So the historian, rather like the modern student of race-awareness in young children, must remain tentative and baffled as to whether white men originally responded adversely to the African's color because of strictly accidental prior cultural valuation of blackness, instinctual repulsion founded on physiological processes or perhaps fear of the night which may have had adaptive value in human evolution, or the association of dirt and darkened complexion with the lower classes in Europe (Jordan, 1968, p 257). Blackness was functional in a slave society where white men were masters. It served as an easily grasped symbol of the African's baseness and blackness had become so thoroughly entangled with the basest status in American society that by the eighteenth century it was almost coded into American language and literature. Enslavement of blacks complicated the meaning of color.

The state of inquiry into the meaning of blackness at the beginning of the eighteenth century is illustrated in a passage from a series of brief, chatty, and highly revealing disquisitions which were popular in both England and America.

> Question: Whether Negroes shall rise so at the last Day? Answer: The pinch of the question only lies whether white or black is the better colour? For the Negroes won't be persuaded but their jett is finer and more beautiful than our alabaster. If we paint the devil black, they are even with us, for they paint him white, and no doubt are as much in the right on't as we; none amongst them, who are legitimate, being born white, but such as are a kind of leprous persons. And they boast of an Emperor of Rome, one of the best of 'em ('twas Severus) and Saints, Fathers, and Martyrs without number, who have been of that colour. But after all, unless we are very partial, there is something natural in't. Black is of the colour of night, frightful, dark and horrid; but white of the day and light, refreshing and lovely. Taking then this blackness of the Negro to be an accidental imperfection . . . I conclude thence, that he shall not rise with that complexion, but leave it behind him in the darkness of the grave, exchanging it for a brighter and a better, at his return again into the world (The Athenian Oracle, London, 1704, "cited by" Jordan, 1968, pp 435-36).

In twentieth-century America, few people remember the emperors of Rome, but few people have to be told (though everyone is) that whiteness is "lovely" and "refreshing." In the latter part of the eighteenth century, Americans would find reason to regard their own whiteness as integral to their emergence as an enlightened nation, into "a brighter and a better" though a less spiritual "world."

Chapter Three will deal with the positive image of blackness. Poets of the Harlem Renaissance gave rise to this positive feeling through their writings which exalted the color "black."

Chapter Three

THE POSITIVE IMAGE OF BLACKNESS

Living under the conditions of slavery, many blacks came to the point of losing faith in themselves. They came to feel that perhaps they were less than human. The great tragedy of physical slavery was that it led to mental slavery. Then something happened to blacks. Circumstances made it necessary for them to travel more. Rural plantation life was gradually replaced by migration to urban and industrial communities. The economic life of blacks was gradually rising and through the decline of illiteracy, the cultural life of blacks took on a new dimension. These factors caused blacks to take a new look at themselves. Black masses began to re-evaluate themselves. They came to feel that they were somebody. Their religion revealed that God loves all of His children, and that every man is significant. As one poet put it:

> Fleecy locks and black complexion
> Cannot forfeit nature's claim.
> Skin may differ, but affection
> Dwells in black and white the same.
>
> And were I so tall as to reach the pole
> Or to grasp the ocean at a span,
> I must be measured by my soul.
> The mind is the standard of the man
> (Knig, 1957, p 25).

The Black Renaissance gave rise to a positive feeling of blackness. This black presence became felt at the middle of the nineteenth century. The 1848 abolition of the slave trade gave rise to this movement and that date can be considered a landmark in the Black Renaissance movement. Before then, the black man's conception of self was always based on comparison with that of whites. In the words of William Du Bois in Souls of Black Folk:

> After the Egyptian and Indian, the Greek and Roman, the Teuton and Mongolian, the Negro is a sort of seventh son, born with a veil, and gifted with second sight in this American world a world which yields him no true self-consciousness but only lets him see himself through the revelation of the other world. It is a peculiar sensation, this double-consciousness, this sense of always looking at one's self through the eyes of others, of measuring one's soul by the tape of a world that looks on in amused contempt and pity.

and in James Weldon Johnson's poem "O Black and Unknown Bards":

> O black and unknown bards of long ago,
>   How come your lips to touch the
>   sacred fire?
> How, in your darkness, did you come to
>   know the power and beauty of the
>   minstrel's lyre?
> Who first from midst his bonds lifted
>   his eyes?
> Who first from out the still watch, lone
>   and long,
> Feeling the ancient faith of prophets rise
>   within his dark-kept soul, burst
>   into song?

In that poem a new set of vocabulary is introduced into the literary world. Black, darkness, and similar words suddenly lose their traditional connotation in white literature. Writers in America who hesitated about the new movement were greatly encouraged by the Souls of Black Folk (1903) of Du Bois.

The revelation in vocabulary continued. Countee Cullen in his "Tableau" would refer to the color black as "the sable pride of night" and

Claude McKay would in "The Tropics in New York" tantalize the reader with the luscious freshness of tropical fruits.

> Bananas ripe and green, and ginger root,
> Cocoa in pods and alligator pears,
> And tangerines and mangoes and grapefruit,
> Fit for the highest prize at parish fairs.

In Jean Toomer's <u>Cane</u>, the color black loses its derogatory connotations for slaves are referred to as "dark purple ripened plums, squeezed and bursting in the pine wood air." Blacks were no longer ashamed of their color. They were even ready to exhibit the beauty of black as Langston Hughes in "Jazzonia" published in "The Crisis."

> What jungle tree have you slept under,
>   Midnight dancer of the jazzy hour?
> What great forest has hung its perfume
>   Like a sweet veil about your bower?
> What jungle tree have you slept under,
>   Dark-brown girl of the swaying hips?
> What star-white moon has been your lover?
>   To what mad faun have you offered your lips?

With Countee Cullen's "Heritage," blacks learn to speak with pride. The sun will have the color of copper and black will become the symbol of royalty. The real revolution had been achieved in American literature. It would be up to the future generation to push this revolt to the point of anarchy, a point achieved thirty years later in the sixties, a polarization that will no doubt give rise to a synthesis of ideas, structures and styles (Richards, 1971, p 157).

The dominant note in historical writing when dealing with blacks is to emphasize ideas of self-depreciation and to convey the notion that self-pride is something quite new. The former appears in much of the writing of Eugene Genovese and is central to William Styron's novel <u>The Confessions of Nat Turner</u>; and since professional historians including Genovese, Martin Duberman, and C. Vann Woodward have spoken highly of the authenticity of Styron's work one is uncertain in just that genre it belongs (Aptheker, 1971, p 169). As to the note of discovering something new, an example is Edmund Cronon's useful biography <u>Black Moses: The Story of Marcus Garvey and the Universal Negro Improvement Association</u>:

> ...the racial doctrines of Marcus Garvey were infusing in Negroes everywhere a strong sense of pride in being black. For the first time in the long bitter centuries since their ancestors had left Africa in chains, masses of Negroes in the United States and elsewhere in the New World were glorying in their color.

A historian should be careful in writing "for the first time" or "never." In this case, one wonders what Mr. Cronon would do with the following poem by Du Bois published a generation before Marcus Garvey came to America.

> I am the Smoke King.
> I am black,
> I am darkening with song
> I am hearkening no wrong;
> I will be black as blackness can,
> The blacker the mantle the mightier the man.

One of Du Bois' classics was the <u>Souls of Black Folk</u> that appeared in 1903. Its point was to express "a strong sense of pride in being black," it appeared when whites were publishing books with such titles as <u>The Mystery Solved: The Negro a Beast</u>, and here was a black man writing prose exalting the souls of these animals (Aptheker, 1971, p 170).

Another case in point is W. J. Simmons' <u>Men of Mark: Eminent, Progressive and Rising</u>, in which he expresses this sense of pride and strove to further it. The book was published in 1887 when Simmons was president of the State University in Louisville, Kentucky. In the preface he writes: "I wish the book to show to the world -- to our oppressors and even to our friends -- that the Negro race is still alive, and must possess more intellectual vigor than any other section of the human family. . ."

On the same theme, here are a few lines from a speech written by Dr. John S. Rock from a speech he delivered in Boston in 1858.

> When I contrast the fine, tough muscular system the beautiful, rich color, the full broad features, and the gracefully frizzled hair of the Negro, with the delicate physical organization, wan color, sharp features and long hair of the Caucasian, I am inclined to believe that when the white man was created, nature was pretty well exhausted -- but, determined to keep up appearances, she pinched up his features, and did the best she could under the circumstances.

This can be compared with the essay that Du Bois published in Mencken's magazine "The Smart Set," in April 1923, entitled "The Superior Race." It was written in the form of a Socratic dialogue between Du Bois and his "white friend."

This "white friend" is startled to find Du Bois saying that "in faces I hate straight features; needles and razors may be sharp -- but beautiful, never." While Du Bois consoles his friend that as such matters are simply "personal opinions" and "matters of taste," he goes on to express his own tastes; he chooses, he says, "intricately curly hair, black eyes, full and luscious features, and that air of humility and wonder that streams from moonlight." He continues: "Add to this, voices that caress instead of rasp, glances that appeal rather than repel, and a sinuous litheness of movement to replace Anglo-Saxon stalking there you have my ideal."

Du Bois ends up by telling his "friend": "Can you not see that I am laughing at you?" Do you not understand that the world of human beings is not "simply a great layer cake with superimposed slices of inferior and superior races, interlaid with mud?"

And he adds:

> All that I have really been trying to say is that a certain group that I know and to which I belong, as contrasted with the group you know and to which you belong, and in which you fanatically and glorifyingly believe, bears in its bosom just now the spiritual hope of this land because of the persons who compose it and not by divine command.

The poets of the Harlem Renaissance period in the 1920s often conveyed a sense of black superiority. Countee Cullen writes;

> My love is dark as yours is fair
> Yet lovlier I hold her
> Than listless maids with pallid hair,
> And blood that thin and colder

And Gwendolyn Bennett I also in the 1920s:

> I love you for your browness
>   And the rounded darkness of
>   your breast;
> I love you for the breaking sadness
> in your voice
> And shadows where your way-ward
> eye-lids rest (Aptheker, 1971, p 178).

The work of these artists are the direct opposite of Harvey Swados' "self-underestimation and self-depreciation."

Chapter Four will discuss the savage image of Africa portrayed in the movies, textbooks, cartoons, etc. This negative image along with the way that black was used further enforced the negative aspect of blackness. There are pros and cons concerning the way that black Americans reacted to this stereotyping. Some authors feel that most blacks experienced self-hatred as a result of this practice, while others feel that only a very small portion of the black population was affected. Both sides will be represented.

Chapter Four

PSYCHOLOGICAL EFFECTS

The very word "black" had been synonymous with something evil in the past. Blacks had been programmed to view and think of the world as being non-black, anti-black or the opposite of black. Their world view was dominated by the Euro-American determinants. The sociological, political, cultural, and physiological conditioning that resulted in this world view appeared to be the same for both the working class and middle class blacks. While the content of black experience within the class system differed in some ways, it was similar in that all classes tended to think and behave in a manner that degraded blackness. It was believed that blacks came from a strange, uncivilized, "dark" continent; that black history only began in 1865; and that slavery had acted as a civilizing experience (Copeland, 1971, P 241).

Blacks had been taught the white concept of beauty: thin lips, straight hair, light skin. This concept of beauty attached to whiteness was so deeply ingrained that it was a monster to attack. Throughout the history of the American black, he has been taught that "blackness" is evil, and black is "no-good," and only "white is right," that blacks with "white blood" in their veins were better, as Alvin F. Poussaint points out in his article in The Black Power Revolt.

> The most damaging result of this brainwashing has been that blacks (some) have adopted his self-image from the dictates of whites. We have a long history of blacks learning to hate themselves because of their blackness. It has been shown that the self-concepts of children are formed at a very early age, from their own experiences and their relationships to their environments. The negative self-concept takes hold early in life; if it is not

guarded against, the child evidences it in his expressions, his art, his vocabulary and his entire life style.

The current strains which are bursting forth from sensitized blacks in this country are not new in the sense that they are original. Such concepts as black equality, black unity, black expression, black history, black purpose were all voiced before by such outstanding men as Frederick Douglass, Martin R. Delaney, Henry M. Turner, Edward Blyden, and George W. Williams. The important difference between these men and the black leaders of our time is that the latter are advantageously placed in a time period when widespread, well-planned, Afro-American Studies programs are accepted and encouraged.

The view that blacks in the United States were all ashamed of Africa until the end of World War II is part of the mythology of black American history. There is an abundance of evidence to prove that in the early days, black Americans retained feelings for their ancestral continent. Such evidence shows the long interest of American blacks in Africa, especially the Negro church missions and the Negro church-related colleges education of African students going back into the nineteenth century. Then there is the "back to Africa" emigration movement of the slavery years and continuing up to our own time, as well as the inclusion of the word "African" in early black organizations, such as the "African Methodist Episcopal Church," "African Episcopal Zion Church," the "African Benevolent Society" of Boston, the "Free African Society" of Philadelphia, the "African Masonic Lodge" of Boston, and others. On March 26, 1827, in its opening editorial, Freedoms Journal, the first black newspaper published here in the United States, listed among its objectives: "Useful knowledge of every kind and everything that relates to Africa shall find a ready admission into our columns; and as that vast continent becomes daily more known, we trust that many things will come to light, proving that the natives of it are neither so ignorant nor stupid as they have generally been supposed to be." Many mid-nineteenth century black Americans partly to refute the proslavery argument that Africa had contributed nothing to civilization proudly argued that man's earliest civilizations were in Africa, that the ancient Egyptians were a Negroid or partly black race, and that from Egypt, through Greece and Rome, stemmed all Western civilization. Hence, while the ancestors of the supposedly superior Anglo-Saxons were roaming the forests of northern Europe as savages, Africa had already created the foundations of Western culture (Foner, 1975, p 20).

In 1858 in Cleveland, a book was published entitled A Colored Man Around the World. It was anonymously signed "By A Quadroon," but the author was probably David F. Dorr, a fugitive slave who had made a three year tour of three continents in 1851 and had kept a diary. During his visit to Egypt, he wrote in his diary: "When Thebes had one hundred gates undecayed, she could send to war two millions of men. Such were Egyptian kings of olden time, though black." And again: "Egypt was a higher sphere of artistical science than any other nation on earth. This will naturally convey an idea to the world that the black man was the first skillful animal on the earth, because Horner describes the Egyptians as men with wooly hair, thick lips, flat feet, and black, and we have no better authority than Horner" (Foner, 1975, P 20).

In its issue of August 13, 1865, the New Orleans Daily Tribune, the first black daily newspaper published in the United States, sharply criticized students of antiquity for failing to point out "the African origin of most of our simplest tools, arts and trades." Even if one granted that the Egyptians were "not a pure black race," but "a mixed people," the evidence was clear that the Egyptians "received the first elements of their useful knowledge from the Ethiopians who were pure blacks." In general:

> History shows . . . that the first tools of the useful arts, the first practices of trade and commerce, and the first implements of agriculture, were by an African and black people -- the Ethiopians. It is therefore entirely wrong to say that Africa did not contribute to the great work of civilization, since the black race of Africa was the promoter and the originator of social progress.

Of modern Africa, the Africa from which their ancestors had come, most of these nineteenth-century black Americans said little. There were a few exceptions like Martin R. Delany and several others who visited West Africa in the 1850s and wrote honest accounts of the region and its people. But most black Americans absorbed the conception of whites that modern Africa was savage. Under the influence of endless propaganda in geography and history textbooks, in missionary tales, and later in Tarzan and H. Ridder Haggard novels and movies, all emphasizing the supposedly barbarous and uncivilized condition of Africa, most black Americans turned against their own past and spurned their African heritage as unworthy of attention (Foner, 1975, p 21).

It is true that the influence of Woodson, Du Bois, and Marcus Garvey caused a number of black Americans of the post-World War I generation to draw strength from their African heritage. But even this did not overcome the impact of the stereotype of "savage Africa" presented in motion pictures, cartoons, textbooks, and periodicals. So long as the concept of Africans as savage and primitive survived, most black Americans either were ashamed of their association with Africa or were entirely indifferent to it (Foner, 1975, p 22). Evans puts it this way:

This is not to suggest that the phenomenon of self-hatred does not exist for some individual black people. However, I do not believe that wholesale imputation of this tendency to black people as a group, or even a substantial percentage of them, is justifiable (Evans, 1971).

A black psychologist, Thomas J. Edwards, gives this account of adaptive inferiority. "The first collection circa the late 1920s. This recollection begins with lines from The Song of Solomon.

> I am black, but comely,
>   O daughters of Jerusalem,
> Like the tents of Kedar,
>   Like the curtains of Solomon,
> Do not gaze at me because I am swarthy,
>   Because the sun has scorched me.
> My mother's sons were angry with me,
>   They made me keeper of the vineyards;
> But, my own vineyard I have not kept!

When I was a child in Sunday School (I grew up in the African Methodist Episcopal Church), we would be called on to read a verse from the Bible, and at times someone in a mischievous mood would read this passage from the Song of Solomon. Invariably there would be giggles and snickering. Sometimes the reading had a pointed meaning for a fumbling teacher who was not too well liked and who may have been dark besides. Her black students would take hostile delight in her embarrassment. But whether or not this was the case, these lines would always generate awkward amusement in the class. When the reading was finished, the teacher without further comment would call on the next child while the giggles subsided. The words "black" and "swarthy" in those days had self-reference implications that we could handle only in jest or in anger, or a combination of both; and the concept of their being

related to comeliness or beauty was absurd! Black was
not beautiful, and neither were we (Pugh, 1972, p 18).

A number of writers (Curry, 1964; Hamilton, 1966; Sterba, 1947; Rodgers, 1955) have pointed out the symbolic associations that cluster around the colors black and white in our western culture. White is most often associated with cleanliness, divinity, illumination, purity, goodness, awareness, life, knowledge, and heaven. Black is associated with the mysterious, the exotic, the savage, dirt, sin, badness, inferiority, darkness, sleep, death, emotional abandon, man's fallen state, evil, ignorance, the unconscious, power, magic, libido, Hades, Judas, and Satan. Psychoanalysts dealing with the fantasies of white clients about blacks have noted the frequency with which such fantasies disclose an unconscious identification between the black male and the oedipal father (Sterba, 1947; Rodgers, 1955) and the unwanted sibling (Sterba, 1947) the phallic-sadistic rapist (Rodgers, 1955), and the indulging, uncritical manny (Grier, 1967). These observations can be documented in the associations, fantasies, and dreams produced by white clients in treatments with black therapists (Pugh, 1972, p 45).

The youngsters of the 1960s, reversed the psychology of rejection and self-abnegation with the counter-psychology of beautiful blackness and self-love (Banks & Grambs, 1972, p 38).

As most of the older studies indicate, it is common for white and black social scientists to write and reiterate that black people, in general, have a negative self-concept. Even if this were true, it is a defeating frame of reference for a whole group of people. White Anglo-Saxon Protestants have never allowed the above to begin. Whites have constantly, and emphatically denied it through their own writers of fiction, nonfiction, psychology, sociology, and politics, and they have done this for a very good reason. The fact of continued and widespread emphasis is in itself negating. Continued repetition will, and has in the case of blacks, crystallize negative attitudes of teachers toward children and their home conditions, politicians toward their black constituents, psychologists' and psychiatrists' interpretations of data from their patients, other social scientists toward their subjects, and literary writers toward their protagonists (Banks & Grambs, 1972, p 96).

Foremost is the effort to make blacks believe that they have a negative self-concept by repeatedly writing about it. This negativism is revealed in studies on the black self-concept from Goodman (1946) to Morland (1966), on how blacks hate themselves.

Another effort to negate blacks is the way the English language serves to denigrate blackness. As Ossie Davis pointed out, a superficial examination of Roget's Thesaurus of the English Language reveals 120 synonyms for blackness. They include "blot, blotch, slight, smut, smug, sully, begrime, soot, becloud, obscure, dingy, murky, threatening, frowning, foreboding, forbidding, sinister, baneful, dismal, wicked, malignant, deadly, unclean, dirty, unwashed, and foul." Included in the same listing were words such as "Negro, negress, nigger, and darkey." On the other hand Davis found 134 synonyms for the word "white," almost all of them with favorable connotations expressed in such words as "purity, cleanness, immaculateness, bright, shiny, clean, clear, chaste, unblemished, innocent, just, straightforward, fair, and genuine."

Podair emphasizes Davis' point by stressing that there is a link between language patterns and race relations. The English language stereotypes blacks, thereby intensifying race prejudice. It shapes ideas, concepts, and attitudes about people. Podair insists that the points of view, expressed in "dark house," "black," "black sheep," and "black and white," are difficult to counteract and, therefore, should be of import to the social scientists working in the area of race relations (Banks & Grambs, 1972, p 98).

Margaret Burroughs' poem "What Shall I Tell My Children Who Are Black" further clarifies the subtle psychological effort to make blacks hate themselves through the use of standard English:

> They are faced with abhorrence of every-
> thing that is black.
> The night is black and so is the
> boogyman.
> Villains are black with black hearts.
> A black cow gives no milk. A black
> hen lays no eggs.
> Bad news comes bordered in black,
> mourning clothes black,
> Storm clouds, black, black is evil
> And evil is black and devils food
> is black
>
> What shall I tell my dear ones
> raised in a white world.
> A place where white has been made
> to represent
> All that is good and pure and
> fine and decent,
> Where clouds are white and dolls,
> and heaven
> Surely is a white, white place with
> angels
> Robed in white, and cotton candy and
> ice cream
> And mild and ruffled Sunday dresses
> And dream houses and long sleek
> Cadillacs
> And angel's food is white . . .all,
> all . . . white (Burroughs, 1968).

Blacks have always had a mass positive self-concept. For instance, the Uncle Tomming showed a love of self, for it enabled blacks to continue to live. The severity of black mothers with their sons revealed this love of self to perceptive people, who understood that when black mothers forced their sons to be Uncle Toms it was done in order to "raise them." The use of these and other survival techniques during slavery and after suggest the love of self of blacks. Since a hatred of self could have led to an almost total destruction of the black race in America, the existence of thirty million blacks in this country today suggests a love of self in blacks (Banks & Grambs, 1972, p 102).

Although Kardiner and Ovesey (1966), declared that self-hatred is demonstrated when black males use hair-processing techniques to deny a black attribute, it is the reverse that is true. This hair-processing technique is used to heighten masculinity. It is, as Keil says:

> The hair-processing techniques that Abrahams finds "reminiscent of the handkerchief typing of Southern Mammies" are designed to heighten masculinity. Backstage at the Regal Theatre in Chicago "process rags" are everywhere in evidence among the male performers, the same performers who put the women in the audience into states that border on the ecstatic. Prettiness (wavy hair, manicured nails, frilly shirts, flashy jackets) plus strength, tender but tough. This is the style that many black women find irresistible. A blues singer is not unconsciously mimicking Elvis Presley's hairdo (the opposite may be true) or Aunt Jemima's when he straightens his hair and keeps it in place with a kerchief. He is enhancing his sex appeal nothing more (Keil, 1967, p 27).

Recently, there are new insights into the role of the black mothers in their effect on the masculinity of the black male. The negativism of the

Moynihan Report of 1965 on the black family is again being challenged in a recent discussion of black manhood. This report suggests that there is no lack of a male image and that, in addition, females also instruct male children in the expectations of the typical behavior of men, according to their experience of man-woman relationships (Mannerz, pp 16-21).

Now that blacks have rejected the theories of cultural deprivations and cultural disadvantagement, white-oriented social scientists are endeavoring to prove that blacks lack of success in America is due to their negative self-concept rather than to the racist nature of society and its exclusionary institutions and methods (Banks & Grambs, 1972).

The myriad of negative symbols conjured up by the white society served as the locus for developing a different statement of self-hood. The concept that "black is beautiful" is merely the overt manifestation of the deeper process of trying on new, and previously denied, role patterns. The research by the Clarks makes it very clear that black youngsters in the past did not consider black as being beautiful. This research was conducted prior to the beginning of what is commonly referred to as the black revolution. The period of the sixties has seen an explosion of black pride which will have significance for the future development of black identity (Banks & Grambs, 1972).

Blacks today are defining themselves. Having discarded the meaningless name, Negro, they are saying, "I'm black and I'm proud." The demands for black literature and black history are attempts at restructuring the temporal-spatial arrangements of history to accommodate the presence and past of other pseudospecies, to remove the constraints on the dissemination and distribution of knowledge, and to permit the installation of the worth of blackness as a value in the black community (Wyne, White, & Coop, 1974).

Natural Afro hair styles, dashikis, "uhuru," and "umoja" are symbols of this value-building effort. Black consciousness is rapidly being developed. For many, the traditional stereotype of the Sambo image has been rejected and in its place there is a positive stereotype, "black is beautiful." Black has made a dramatic change from something that was bad to be avoided, to a badge of intense pride.

The most important explanation lies in what has happened to the word "black" in the past few years. Black is now beautiful, and it is beautiful to be black. There has emerged a new feeling of pride in blackness and the distinctive characteristics of the black culture are manifested in black pride (Wyne, White, Coop, 1974, p 89).

Black Americans today are more concerned with their relationship to Africa than at any time in our history. Many today realize that their attitude toward Africa has been the result of what Philip Curtin calls, "cultural arrogance," which is based upon the concept of the superiority of Western ways and thoughts. They are also aware that Africa, long considered the Dark Continent, has a history reaching back to the very dawn of human consciousness; that ancient Africans long considered primitive and ignorant, had their own highly developed cultures; and that for thousands of years Africa has contributed to the development of human civilization.

The growth of the black community and the creation of an essentially autonomous black sub-culture were the most important developments of the Afro-American experience to 1865, and these developments would have a profound effect on the subsequent course of black history. Because Afro-American slaves retained a positive self-image and continued to see themselves as a "moral people" they were able not only to survive in slavery, but to transcend the institution that bound them, bequeathing to their posterity and to the world a unique example of survival and creativity in the face of extreme adversity.

Chapter Five focuses upon symbolism. A large portion of this chapter is concerned with the symbolism of the two colors, black and white and the way that they are used in the Bible. A smaller portion of this section discusses the negative connotation of black in the writings of Shakespeare, and to a lesser degree, other English writers. Also included are the connotations of black and white in other cultures.

Chapter Five

SYMBOLISM

In coming to terms with himself, every black individual has had in one way or another to cope with the infinity of ways in which white is elevated above black in our culture. The association of white and black with light and dark and the translation of these quantities of light into polarities of good and evil and beauty and ugliness has taken place in the conventions and languages of many cultures, but in few has this conversion of physical facts into religious and aesthetic values been worked harder than in the Anglo world.

These concepts and usages of black evil and white goodness, of beautiful fairness and ugly blackness, are deeply imbedded in the Bible, are folded into the language of Milton and Shakespeare, indeed are laced into almost every entwining strand of the art and literature in which our history is clothed. They can be traced down the columns of any dictionary from white hope to whitewash, from the black arts to the Black Mass, from black-browed and black-hearted to blacklist and blackmail (Isaacs, 1963).

The Bible's central theme of good and evil is constantly represented by the symbolism of black and white and dark and light. In the Scriptures the use of "black" as a negative word is consistent throughout, standing for sin, ignorance, wickedness and evil. "My skin is black," cries Job using this figure to show how heavy was his burden of sin. Again in Job: "Let darkness and the shadow of death stain it; let a cloud dwell upon it; let the blackness of the day terrify it." Or in Jeremiah: "For this shall the earth mourn and the heavens above be black." And in the Epistle of Jude the famous phrase about "the wandering stars to whom is reserved the blackness of darkness forever."

The word "white" is apparently used a good deal less in the Bible, and less consistently. "The great white throne" of God in Revelation, the "white raiments" of the elders in Judges. But "white," though most often signifying beauty, purity and elegance, is also more rarely used as a literally descriptive word in connection with Leprosy, and has been associated in the language with pestilence and death. More consistent is the juxtaposition of "light" and "dark," the dark being always bad and light always good, from the original creation of light to divide it from the primeval dark and to show the way for men to see truth and good works and glory and the light of God himself: "In Thy light," sang the Psalmist, "shall we see light." There can be no question that when the Lord looked upon his work and found it good, it was the light that pleased him, not the dark. Where the references occur in the Bible to a literal blackness of skin, the association seems to retain its negative cast. "Look not upon me, because I am black." There is also the reference to skin color in Numbers when the Lord is angry at Aaron and Miriam after they had spoken against Moses for marrying "an Ethiopian woman," the term "Ethiopian" signifying a person of black skin. The text suggests that the Lord was angry primarily because the offenders were jealous of Moses' special role as the Lord's man. His punishing finger touched Miriam and she became, "leprous, white as snow" (Baxter & Sansom, "cited by" Isaacs, 1972, pp 146-47). It is Isaacs' contention that Aaron was objecting to the Ethiopian woman not because she was black but because she was gentile. It is also his belief that the Israelites were not a white race.

Christianity has been accompanied by a symbolism of color. This symbolism has formed and cultivated a sensitivity to color that extends even to people who claim to be detached from religion. It has created a "backwash" of fixed impressions and attitudes difficult to efface.

Racial hatred has not evolved solely from this Christian symbolism; nor can it be fully explained by economic causes alone. Its roots extend much farther and deeper. They reach into sexual complexes and into religion through the symbolism of color (Bastide, 1968, p 36).

When Christians tried to justify slavery, they claimed black skin was a punishment from God. They invoked the curses cast upon Cain, the murderer of his brother I and upon Ham, son of Noah, who had found his drunken father naked in his tent. Against the background of this symbolism, they invented causes for the malady, intended to justify in their own eyes a process of production based upon the exploitation of black labor. Later, other rationalizations and counter rationalizations got woven around the same symbolism.

The Christian symbolism of color is very rich. Medieval painting makes full use of it. Some colors are more pertinent than others. The color yellow has come to signify treason. When Westerners think of Asians, they unconsciously transpose this significance to them, converting it into a trait of ethnic psychology. Consequently, they treat Asians as persons in whom they cannot have confidence. They can, of course, give excellent reasons in defense of their behavior; the closed or uncommunicative character of the Japanese, the smiling impassiveness of the Chinese, or some historic case of treason. These are all reasons invented after the fact. If Westerners could have prevented themselves from being influenced by a symbolism centuries old, they could just as easily found reasons to justify an impression of the yellow race as loyal and affectionate (Bastide, 1968, p 36).

But the greatest Christian two-part division is that of white and black. White is used to express the pure, while black expressed the diabolical. The conflict between Christ and Satan, the spiritual and the carnal, good and evil came finally to be expressed by the conflict between white and black, which underlines and synthesizes all the others. Even the blind, who know only night, think of a swarm of angels or of devils in association with white and black. For example, "a black soul," "the blackness of an action," "a dark deed," "the innocent whiteness of the lily," "to bleach someone of a crime." These are not merely adjectives and nouns. Whiteness brings to mind the light, ascension into the bright realm, the immaculateness of virgin snow, the white dove of the Holy Spirit, and the transparency of limpid air; blackness suggests the infernal streams of the bowels of the earth, the pit of hell, the devil's color (Bastide, 1968, p 37).

This dichotomy became so dominant that it dragged certain other colors along with it. Celestial blue became a simple satellite of white in painting the cloak of the Immaculate Virgin, while the red flames of hell became a fit companion for the darkest colors. Thinking is so enslaved to language that this chain of associated ideas operates automatically when a Caucasian finds himself in contact with a black person. Mario de Andrade has rightly exposed the evils of this Christian symbolism as being rooted in the very origins of the prejudice of color (Bastide, 1968, p 37).

The entire history of Western painting bears witness to the deliberate whitening or bleaching effort that changed Christ from a Semitic to an Aryan person. The dark hair that Christ was thought to have had came to be rendered as very light-colored, and his dark eyes as blue. It was necessary that he be as far removed as possible from everything that could suggest darkness or blackness, even indirectly. His hair and his beard were given the color of sunshine, the brightness of the light above, while his eyes retained the color of the sky (Bastide, 1968).

The progressive Aryanization of Christ is in strict accordance with the logic of the color symbolism. It did not start until Christianity came into close contact with the other races, with the Africans race in particular. Christian artists began to avoid the darker tints in depicting Christ in order to remove as much as possible of their evil suggestion.

The Middle Ages did have their famous Black Madonnas which were and still are the object of a devotion perhaps even deeper than that which is dedicated to many of the fair complexioned images of the Holy Virgin. But the Black Virgin represents to her devotees not so much the Loving Mother as a sorceress, a rain maker, a worker of miracles. She has the magnetism of the strange, smacking of Gypsies and Moors; she stirs the heart as if a bit of magic, even a near-diabolical sorcery, were involved in her miracles. She is not the beloved mother who clasps the unfortunate to her breast and comforts them, but a mysterious goddess endowed with extraordinary powers. The symbolism of her dark color is not eliminated in the cult; it is only repressed. The Black Virgin helps one to understand the appeal used by Catholicism in its efforts to convert "pagan peoples" to the faith (Bastian, 1968).

References must again be made to painting. The Three Kings who came to worship the newborn child were depicted as white men at first. Later they came to represent Africa, Asia, and Europe. Balthasar was the black king who came to bring his tribute to the babe. He was pictured behind the other two Magi and even sometimes kneeling closest to the

Babe, but never between the other two. That would have been equivalent to ignoring his color. Racism subsisted in the disguised form of a patronizing attitude in this first attempt to remove the demoniac symbolism from the black skin (Bastide, 1938, p 38).

A similar effort can be seen in the creation of black saints intended for races other than the white race. St. Mauritius, a commander of the Roman legions in Egypt who was martyred there, was originally depicted as white but then as a Moor, and finally in the thirteenth century as an African.

Such changes were exploited for purposes of evangelism as the frontiers of the known world extended farther. The church long ignored St. Benedict of Palermo, known as St. Benedict the Moor, but finally officialized him with the development of missions in Africa and of slavery in the Western Hemisphere. This case illustrates another rationalization on the part of the church intended to break the nominal chain of symbolism. In order to escape from feminine temptations, St. Benedict prayed to God to make him ugly, so God turned his skin black (Bastide, 1968).

The black saints St. Mauritius, St. Benedict the Moor, St. Iphigenia the Mulatto, and St. Balthasar the black king are only intermediaries, well below the Virgin Mary and Christ who stayed white. They express more the difference, the abyss, between people of different races than the unity. They stand for stratification in a multi-racial society. The color black found only a subordinate place in the hierarchy descending from white to black.

Blacks set out to reverse the values of the traditional Catholic iconographic system. They first invented black angels with African hair and flat noses. Then, prompted by a sentence in the Gospels referring to the Holy Virgin, Niger erat sed pulchara ("Black she was, but beautiful"), they conceived of a Black Virgin. This happened only in comparatively recent times. Christ himself was left untouched, as though to make him black would have been a sacrilege. Paternalism was still too strong for the hierarchy of color to be upset entirely.

Only in a country where segregation became the rule, as in Anglo-Saxon, Protestant North America and African colonies, did the revolt of the blacks go so far as to create a Black God and a Black Christ. In the African colonies, Messianism represented an effort on the part of Africans to free themselves from the dominance to the white missions and to establish Black Messiahs as saviors of their own race (Bastide, 1968).

The Protestant's association of the color black with evil and sin was as strong as the Catholic's. But the Protestant, feeling sure that his soul would go straight to hell, placed the bulwark of Puritanism between himself and the temptation of the woman with color-tinted skin (Bastide, 1968, p 4.1).

Dark skin came to symbolize both in Africa and in America, the abandonment of a race in sin. The symbolism of color took on one of the most complicated and subtle forms, in both Protestantism and Catholicism, through the various steps through which darkness of color became associated with evil itself.

In the symbolic association of color which have been discussed, some of the elements have disappeared. Associations with the devil and sin have no place in the concept of the universe introduced in the late-nineteenth century. Black and white have taken on other meanings. These meanings still follow the basic antithesis founded centuries before on the white purity of the elect and the blackness of Satan. Because this symbolism became secularized, it survived the collapse of the old Christian code of ethics and the advent of another system of ideas. A change of polarization is taking place today. The conflict between light and dark is not so much expressed by the two colors black and white, as by a chain of experience of white men in their relations with races of non-European stock. A black or dark color has come to symbolize a certain social situation, class, or caste. The carry-over of the Bible's imagery into the common usage, visible in Chaucer and Milton, is illustrated in Shakespeare, whose own impact on the English language has hardly been less great than that of the Bible itself.

> Black is the badge of hell,
> The hue of the dungeons and the
> suit of night.

says the king in Love's Labour's Lost, in a passage of raillery in which the beauty of Rosaline is called "black as ebony" and her admirer Biron chided for loving "an Ethiope." In quite another tone, in Macbeth, "The devil damn thee black," again the symbolic joining of sin, the devil and the blackness of skin which runs continuously from Job and the prophets through centuries of Western literature. (Fitzgerald in Omar Khayyam; "For all the sin wherewith the face of man is blackened . . .") In Shakespeare's first tragedy, Titus Andronicus, the villain is a black man. In Othello, Shakespeare treats the theme with greater subtlety. No doubt is left that Brabantio's rage is due in part of the thought that his daughter would run "to the sooty bosom as such a thing as thou," but the direct allusions to Othello's color are few. The most ironic are those Shakespeare puts in the mouth of Othello himself, as where in the rage of his rising jealousy he says:

> Her name that was as fresh
> as Dian's visage is now begrimed and
>   black
> As mine own face.

And where he cries out: "Arise, black vengeance!" He looks

upon the sleeping Desdemona not wanting to shed her blood,

> Nor scar that whiter skin of hers than
>   snow
> And smooth as monumental alabaster.

When he has done the deed, the servant Emilia shrieks at him, "You the

blacker devil!"

In Hollywood, the tradition requires cowboy heroes always to wear a

white hat and ride a white horse and cowboy villains always a black hat

and a black horse.

These themes of blackness and whiteness as expressed in Shakespeare

can be pursued deeper as Professor Harry Levin did in <u>The Power of</u>

<u>Blackness</u>, in which he examines the imagery of black and blackness in

Hawthorne, Poe and Melville.

William Blake's poem, The Little Black Boy published in 1789, is on

this same theme.

> My mother bore me in the southern wild,
> And I am black, but O! my soul is white;
> White as an angel is the English child,
> But I am black, as if bereav'd of light.
> My mother . . . began to say:
>
> . . And we are put on earth a little space
> That we may learn to bear the beams of love;
> And these black bodies and this sunburnt face
> Is but a cloud, and like a shady grove.
> For when our souls have learn'd the heat to bear,

> The cloud will vanish; we shall hear His voice,
> Saying: "Come out from the grove, My love and
> care,
> And round my golden tent like lambs rejoice."
> Thus did my mother say, and kissed me;
> And thus I say to little English boy.
> When I from flack and he from white cloud free,
> I'll shade him from the heat, till he can bear
> To lean in joy upon our Father's knee;
> And then I'll stand and stroke his silver hair,
> And be like him, and he will then love me
> (Baxter and Sansom, 1972, p 149).

The raising of white and debasement of black has been marked deep on the minds of all through time in the Western world. Like the English child in Blake's poem, he was already the color of angels, while the black man could only yearn after whiteness, whether of character, soul, or of skin, and hope that by becoming like whites, whether on earth or in heaven, he would come at last to be loved. This arrangement of things was communicated to all in our culture by all its modes and means, passed by osmosis through all the membranes of class, caste and color of relationships, caressingly and painlessly injected into our children by their school texts and storybooks.

A contemporary example, out of the Doctor Dolittle stories, is written by an Englishman. Doctor Dolittle goes to Africa to cure monkeys of a plague. Dolittle and his animal helpers become the prisoners of a black king. In the king's garden the parrot and the monkey meet the king's son, Prince Bumpo, who is pictured as an ugly-gnome-like black man with a large nose that covers most of his face. They hear him yearn aloud: "If only I were a white prince!" The parrot promises that Doctor Dolittle will change his color if he helps them to escape. To Doctor Dolittle, the unhappy prince tells his story:

> Years ago I went in search of The Sleeping Beauty, whom I had read of in a book. And having travelled through the world many days, I at last found her and kissed the lady very gently to wake her as the book said I should. "Tis true indeed that she woke. But when she saw my face she cried out, "Oh he's black!" And she ran away and wouldn't marry me but went to sleep again somewhere else. So I came back, full of sadness to my father's kingdom. Now I hear that you are a wonderful magician and have many powerful potions. So I come to you for help. If you will turn me white, so that I may go back to The Sleeping Beauty, I will give you half of my kingdom and anything besides you ask.

Bumpo refused to settle just for blond hair and says: "I would like my eyes blue, too, but I suppose that would be very hard to do." The doctor concocts a paste which whitens Bumpo's face and keeps it that way long enough for him and his friends to escape, having first refused to give Bumpo a mirror because he knew that the medicine would wear off and that Bumpo would be "as black as ever in the morning." As they escape, the doctor says, "Poor Bumpo." The parrot says; "Oh, of course he would know we were just joking with him." The duck says: "serve him right if he does turn black again. I hope it is a dark black." Doctor Dolittle decides that instead of apologizing he will send Bumpo some candy when he gets back home.

The imprint on blacks of this whole system of ordering black and white has been seen and experienced by many. Every black person obviously has been called upon to reject or somehow deflect from himself the associations of evil and inferiority so powerfully attached to blackness. They have been called upon to do this under conditions in which their ego was kept under constant assault from all the conditions of life. That so many blacks in every successive generation found the ego strength to meet and resist these identifications is in itself no small miracle. That a large number accepted the white man's images as the truth about themselves is no wonder at all.

While the homogeneity of meaning within the Caucasian-dominated culture of the West is impressive, the possibility that color symbolism may be common across cultural boundaries is even more challenging. The evidence in this case is much more sparse. Some examples include the Chiang, a Sino-Tibetan border people. For them a sacred white stone is a leading feature of worship. The anthropologist studying this culture notes the people's basic tendency to equate white with goodness, and blackness with evil (Torrance, 1933). Among the Mongour, descendants of the Mongols, black is the color of mourning, and white betokens good fortune. The Chuckchees of Siberia utilize black to symbolize the Kelets, or evil spirits. Germaine Dieterlen has observed that for the Bambara, a West African tribe, white is used to symbolize wisdom and purity of the spirit (Dieterlen, 1951). A piece of white cloth is sometimes hung over the door of a home where the inhabitants have just made a sacrifice; white is also the regal color. The dark tones of indigo connote obscenity, impurity, and sadness. Black is also identified with the North and the rainy season. Blacks of Northern Rhodesia are observed to associate good luck with cleanness and whiteness. A hunter smears a white substance on his forehead to invoke the powers of fortune; a person who has met with disaster is said to be "black on the forehead," In Nigeria, the Nupe tribe represents bleak or frightening prospects, sorcery, or evil by black, while white implies luck and good prospects. The Yorubas, also in Nigeria, wear white when worshiping, as they believe the deities prefer white. Among the Creek Indians of North America, white betokens virtue and age, and black implies death. According to Gergen these examinations did reveal irregularities but they were few and limited largely to instances in which white was associated with funeral rites. The major volume of the evidence suggests widespread communality in feeling about black and white.

The primary historic origin of the modern color problem lies in the relation of Europeans to African slavery. It must be recognized that the color theme was first injected into the modern international system by the earlier "Imperial Powers," and that it comprised a major element in the theories with which they legitimized subjecting other peoples to the subordinate, colonial or slave status.

Chapter Six

SUMMARY AND CONCLUSIONS

Throughout the history of this country we have been taught that black is bad. This negative concept takes hold early in life and is evidenced in our art, literature, and our life style. Our modern concept of the color theme was originated by the earlier imperial powers and it comprised a major element in the theories with which they legitimized subjecting other peoples to a subordinate status.

Polarization in terms of color is not an isolated phenomenon. It must be seen in the context of the whole development of western societies and in its relations to the rest of the world.

Studies of color symbolism have concluded that blackness elicits unfavorable responses while white evokes favorable responses. People in advantaged positions tend to ascribe to those of a different color those traits that justify their disadvantaged position. In the culture of the West, color symbolism has served to reinforce the assumptions that whiteness connotes virtue and purity, while blackness connotes wickedness and defilement. The implications of such symbolism for religion and for everyday relations in a society dominated by whites seem obvious. The symbolic meaning of black and white is expressed in most of the major literature of the West. Included are the Bible and the writings of William Shakespeare in which black is used negatively and white positively.

Beginning with the Harlem Renaissance in the 1920s, Du Bois, Countee Cullen and others, exalted blackness in their poems and short stories. Prior to this, other blacks strove to erase the negative stigma attached to blackness. The Harlem Renaissance ushered in a new era of consciousness in which blacks sought to enhance blackness through their literature.

As a result of the savage image of Africa portrayed in the movies, textbooks, cartoons and periodicals, some blacks rejected Africa and blackness. This is not to suggest that all or most blacks experienced self-hatred, rather they rejected the negative portrayal of blackness.

With the advent of the civil rights movement, blackness lost some of its negative connotations. While some words such as blackmail, black ball, black arts, and countless others are still used, blacks themselves are no longer identifying with these negative concepts. They see black in a positive light and as a result of the "black is beautiful" spirit of the 1960s, most blacks now feel that things will never be the same again.

The body of materials for this study has been growing steadily since the 1960s. Of all the great historical developments of the past decade, none has had a more profound impact on the black experience than the emergence of black consciousness. Beginning with the civil rights movement of the late 1950s and gaining in intensity over the years, the sense of black identity, self-awareness and solidarity has given birth to new black values. Black Americans, especially younger blacks, are determined to look on themselves as beautiful, capable, proud and powerful. As their sense of identity and worth has grown, it has created the need for symbolic recognition of that identity, demonstrated in the use of slogans, "black is beautiful," special "Afro" styles of appearance, (the natural haircut, the dashiki), in-group gestures (the power salute, dapping) and adopting the terms "blacks" and "Afro-Americans."

This society does not just think that black is bad. This society is always teaching white superiority. This occurs intuitively, without people thinking about it very much. It occurs in the mass media, in families, in schools, and on television. The American educational system enforces the entrenched values of the society through the use of words. Few people in this country question that this is "the land of the free and the home of the brave." They have heard these words since childhood. Few people question that this is the "great society." We say these things constantly and they become truisms not to be questioned. In a similar way, blacks have been saddled with epithets.

The central problem of blacks here in America is to create an identity for themselves. Solution of this problem seems clearer than it appeared likely only a few years ago. The biggest factor in this change has been the rise of the African states, which is making it possible for blacks here in America to admit their relationship to Africa is encouraging blacks to reconstruct their history and restore the culture ties to Africa that were destroyed by slavery. Since the middle 1950s, Africa has contributed enormously to black self-pride. In the past, Africa contributed to some negative feelings in relationship to the black concept.

Black is still used in a derogatory way, but blacks are not identifying with that concept. They know that they are not what Webster describes. They also know that black has not always been bad or negative and they are no longer seeing themselves in this light. They are beginning to throw off the shackles of inferiority and are beginning to assert themselves in a more positive way.

BIBLIOGRAPHY

1. Banks, James A. and Grambs, Jean D. Black Self-Concept. New York: McGraw-Hill Book Co., 1972.

2. Baughman, Emmett E. Black Americans: A Psychological Analysis. New York: Academic Press, 1971.

3. Bibby, Harold Cyril. Race Prejudice and Education. New York: Prueger, 1959.

4. Bittker, Boris I. The Case For Black Reparations. New York: Random House, 1973.

5. Boyle, Sarah P. Human Beings Only. New York: Leabury Press, 1964.

6. Brigham, John and Weissbach, Theodore. Racial Attitudes in America: Analysis and Findings of Social Psychology. New York: Harper and Row, 1972.

7. Brink, William J. Black and White: A Study of U.S. Attitudes Today. New York: Simon and Schuster, 1967.

8. Brown, William W. The Rising Son. Miami: Mnemosyne Publishing Inc., 1969.

9. Buswell, James Oliver. Slavery, Segregation and Scripture. Grand Rapids: Eerdmans, 1964.

10. Campbell, Byran. American Race Theorists. Boston: Chapmen and Grimes, 1952.

11. Coon, Carleton S. The Living Races of Man. New York: Knopf, 1965.

12. Coop, Richard H., White, Kinnard P., and Wyne Marvin D., The Black Self. Englewood Cliffs: Prentice Hall, Inc., 1974.

13. Cortada, Rafael L. Black Studies. Massachusetts: Xerox College Publishing Co., 1974.

14. De Nevi, Donald P., and Holmes, Doris A. Racism at the Turn of the Century. San Rafael: Leswing Press, 1973.

15. Dorman, James H. and Jones, Robert R. The Afro-American Experience. New York: John Wiley and Sons Inc., 1974.

16. Drimmer, Melvin. Black History. New York: Doubleday and Company Inc., 1968.

17. Ducas, George. Great Documents in Black American History. New York: Praeger Publishing Co., 1970.

18. Dunn, Lynn P. Black Americans. San Francisco: R. and E. Research Associates, 1975.

19. Engerman, Stanley L. and Genovese, Eugene D. Race and Slavery in the Western Hemisphere. Princeton: Princeton University Press, 1975.

20. Firth, Raymond W. Human Types, New York: New American Library, 1958.

21. Fisher, Paul L. and Lowenstein, Ralph. Race and the News Media. New York: Praeger, 1967.

22. Foner, Eric. America's Black Past. New York: Harper and Row Publishers, 1970.

23. Foner, Philip S. The Voice of Black America. New York: Simon and Schuster, 1972.

24. Foner, Philip S. History of Black Americans. Westport: Greenwood Press, 1975.

25. Franklin, John Hope. Color and Race, Boston: Houghton Mifflin Co., 1968.

26. Franklin, John Hope. From Slavery to Freedom. New York: Alfred A. Knopf, 1973.

27. Freimarck, Vincent. Race and the American Romantics. New York: Schocken Books, 1971.

28. Garn, Stanley M. <u>Reading on Race</u>. Springfield: Thomas Co.,
     1960.

29. Golden, James L. and Ricke, Richard D. <u>The Rhetoric of Black
     Americans</u>. Columbus; Charles E. Merrill Publishing Co.,
     1971.

30. Goldsby, Richard A. <u>Race and Races</u>. New York: MacMillan,
     1971.

31. Goldstein, Naomi. <u>The Roots of Prejudice Against the Negro in
     the United States</u>. Boston: Boston University-Press, 1948.

32. Goldstein, Rhoda L. <u>Black Life and Culture in the United States</u>.
     New York: Thomas Y. Crowell Co., 1971.

33. Goldschmid, Marcel L. <u>Black Americans and White Racism</u>. New
     York: Holt, Rinehart and Winston, 970.

34. Gosset, Thomas F. <u>Race</u>, New York: Schocken Books, 1965.

35. Gurin, Patricia and Katz, Irvin. <u>Race and the Social Science</u>. New
     York: Basic Books, 1969.

36. Haller, John S. <u>Outcasts From Evolution</u>. Urbana: University of
     Illinois Press, 1971.

37. Handlin, Oscar. <u>Race and Nationality in American Life</u>. Boston:
     Little Brown, 1957.

38. Hankins, Frank H. <u>The Racial Basis of Civilization</u>. New York: S.
     A. Knopf, 1926.

39. Houston, Baker A. Jr. <u>Long Black Song</u>. Charlottesville: The
     University Press of Virginia, 1972.

40. Huxley, Thomas H. <u>Man's Place in Nature</u>. New York: D.
     Appleton & Co., 1896.

41. Jordan, Winthrop D. <u>White Over Black</u>. Williamsburg: University
     of North Carolina Press, 1968.

42.   Keil, Charles. Urban Blues. Chicago: University of Chicago Press,
       1967.

43.   Kelsey, George D. Racism and the Christian Understanding of
       Man. New York: Scribner Press, 1965.

44.   Klass, Morton. The Kinds of Mankind. Philadelphia: Lippincott,
       1971.

45.   Kovel, Joel. White Racism. New York: Pantheon Books, 1970.

46.   Kuttner, Robert E. Race and Modern Science. New York: Social
       Science Press, 1967.

47.   Lasker, Bruno. Race Attitudes in Children. New York: H. Holt and
       Co., 1929.

48.   Loehlin, John C. Race Differences in Intelligence. San Francisco:
       W. H. Freeman, 1975.

49.   Lloyd, Raymond G. White Supremacy in the U.S. Washington
       Public Affairs Press, 1952.

50.   Mack, Raymond W. Prejudice and Race Relations. Chicago:
       Quadrangle Books, 1970.

51.   McCuen, Gary E. The Racist Reader. Minnesota: Greenhaven
       Press, 1974.

52.   McDonald, Marjorie. Not by the Color of Their Skins. New York:
       International Universities Press, 1971.

53.   Moreland, Lois B. White Racism and the Law. Columbus: Charles
       E. Merrill, 1970.

54.   Newby, Idus A. Jim Crow's Defense: Anti-Negro Thought in
       America, 1900-1930. Baton Rouge: Louisiana State University
       Press, 1965.

55.   Nolen, Claude H. The Negro's Image in the South: The Anatomy
       of White Supremacy. Lexington: University of Kentucky Press,
       1967.

56.   Odum, Howard W. Race and Rumors of Race. Chapel Hills:
      University of North Carolina Press, 1943.

57.   Porter, Judith D. Black Child, White Child: The Development of
      Racial Attitudes. Cambridge: Harvard University Press, 1971.

58.   Pugh, Rodrick W. Psychology and the Black Experience.
      Monterey; Brooks Cole Publishing Co., 1972.

59.   Putnam, Carleton. Framework for Love. Washington: National
      Putnam Letters Committee, 1964.

60.   Richards, Henry J. Topics in Afro-American Studies. New York:
      Black Academy Press, 1971.

61.   Richardson, Ken. Race, Culture and Intelligence. Harmondsworth:
      Penguin Press, 1972.

62.   Robinson, Armstead L. Black Studies in the University. New
      Haven: Yale University Press, 1969.

63.   Snyder, Louis L. The Idea of Racialism: Its Meaning and History.
      Princeton; Van Nostrand, 1962.

64.   Stanton, William. The Leopard's Spots: Scientific Attitudes
      Toward Race in America. Chicago; University of Chicago
      Printing Press, 1960.

65.   Van Eurie, John H. Negroes and Negro Slavery. New York: Smith
      and McDougal, 1861.

66.   Van Eurie, John H. White Supremacy and Negro Subordination.
      New York: Van Eurie, Horton and Co., 1868.

67.   Warren, R. Who Speaks for the Negro. New York: Random
      House, 1966.

68.   Wendel, Earl. This is Race. New York: Shuman, 1950.

69.   Wheat, M. T. The Progress and Intelligence of Americans. Miami:
      Mnemosyne Company, Inc. 1969.

70. Wilcox, Rodger C. The Psychological Consequences of Being a Black American. New York: John Wiley and Sons, Inc., 1971.

71. Wood, Forest G. Black Scare: The Racist Response to Emancipation and Reconstruction. Berkeley: University of California Press, 1968.

72. Wynes, Charles E. Forgotten Voices. Baton Rouge: Louisiana State University Press, 1967.

Magazines, Periodicals, and Journals

1. Editors of Ebony. "The White Problem in America." Ebony, October, 1966.

2. Evarts, Arrah B. "Color Symbolism." Psychoanalytic Review, 1919.

3. Isaacs, Howard R. "Blackness and Whiteness." Encounter, 1963.

4. Pride, Educational Service, Inc. Stevensville: 1971.

5. Williams, J. "Connotations of Racial Concepts and Color Names." Journal of Personality and Social Psychology, 1966.

INDEX

www.ingramcontent.com/pod-product-compliance
Lightning Source LLC
Chambersburg PA
CBHW060632280326
41933CB00012B/2013